Terrific Arctic Terns

Written by Clare Helen Welsh

Collins

The Arctic tern has a sharp, red bill.

It has a dark cap.

This tern feeds on eels.

In winter, it gets dark in the north.
Arctic terns need sunlight.

They go to look for it!

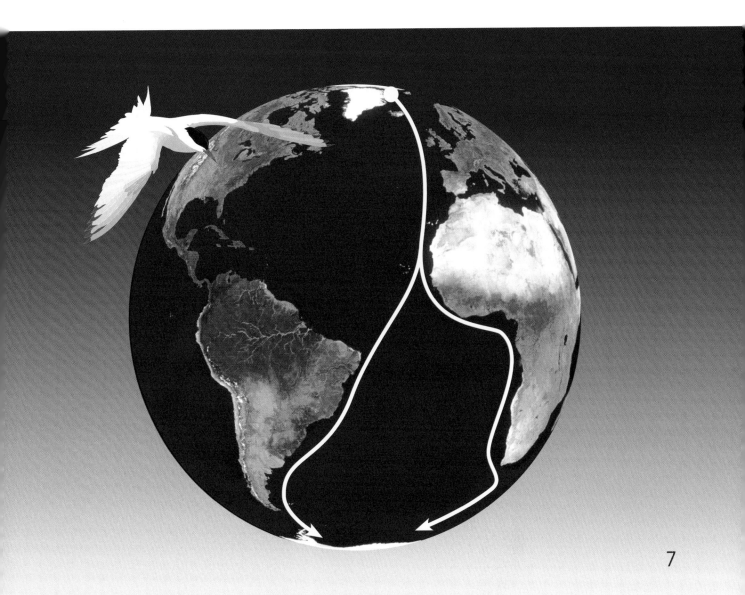

Terns roam far to get to the sunlight.

Then it gets darker.

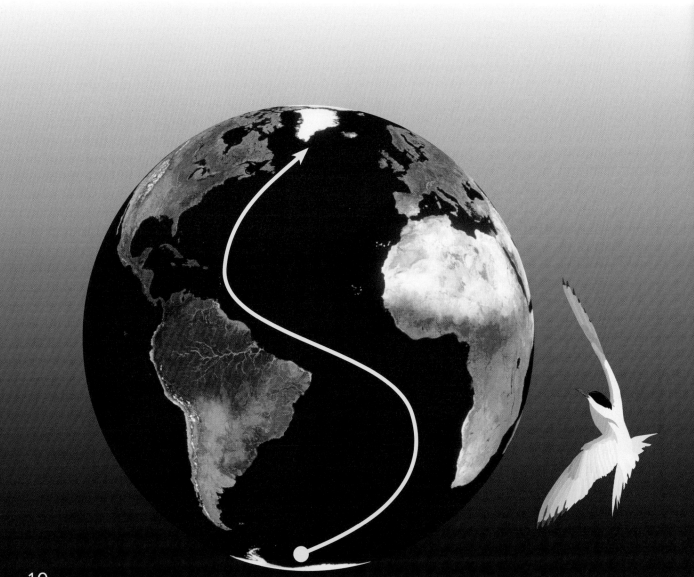

The terns go back north.

The terns are back in the Arctic.

It is summer. For now!

Arctic tern

cap

bill

 Review: After reading

Use your assessment from hearing the children read to choose any GPCs, words or tricky words that need additional practice.

Read 1: Decoding

- Ask the children to read pages 6 and 7. Ask them to work out what the pronouns refer to using the rest of the text:

  page 6: **it** (*the sky/light*)   page 7: **they** (*the Arctic terns*)   **it** (*sunlight*)

- On page 8, ask the children to point to the digraphs and trigraphs in these words:

  terns   **roam**   **far**   **sunlight**

- Ask the children to turn to page 10 and point to the digraph "th" in the word **then**. Now ask them to read the word fluently.

- Challenge the children to choose a page to read fluently to the group. Say: Can you blend in your head when you read the words?

Read 2: Prosody

- Demonstrate a change of pace, reading page 10 more slowly, and speeding up for page 11.
- Discuss why you read page 10 more slowly – to add to the drama of it getting darker.
- Ask the children to take turns reading at different paces to hear, and then discuss, the effects.

Read 3: Comprehension

- Ask the children to look at pages 2 and 3, and compare the Arctic tern with any other birds they are familiar with. In what ways do they look different, or the same?
- Ask the children: What journey do Arctic terns make? (*flying from the north and back*) If necessary turn to pages 7 and 10, and discuss the journey.
- Ask the children to discuss definitions or similar words they could use to explain some of the technical terms:

  page 2: **bill** (e.g. *like a beak, hard pointed mouth*)   page 3: **cap** (e.g. *marking on top of its head*)

  page 4: **feeds** (e.g. *eats, catches and swallows*)   page 8: **roam** (e.g. *fly, travel*)

- Look together at pages 14 and 15. Encourage children to describe the Arctic tern in their own words. Can they name any of the other parts of the bird?